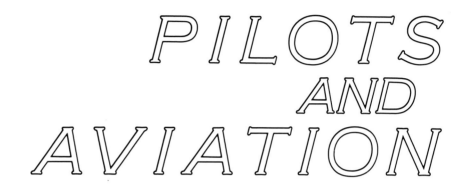

PILOTS AND AVIATION

PILOTS
AND
AVIATION

Carter M. Ayres

Lerner Publications Company
Minneapolis

The author sincerely thanks the following persons and organizations for their valuable contributions: James Callahan, Scott Capener, Cessna Aircraft Company, Experimental Aircraft Association, Future Aviation Professionals of America, Robert Fritsch, Jenna Geiser, Jim Hein, Patty McClain, Rich Morey, Gordon Perkins, Sherry Pottinger, Roger Ritchie, Randy Stoddard-Campen, Konrad Toso, and United Airlines.

To Carole, Andy, and Chris
With Love

Library of Congress Cataloging-in-Publication Data

Ayres, Carter M.
  Pilots and aviation / Carter M. Ayres.
    p. cm.
  Summary: Describes the training and skills necessary to become a pilot and discusses other careers in aviation.
  ISBN 0-8225-1590-3 (lib. bdg.)
  1. Air pilots—Juvenile literature. 2. Aeronautics—Juvenile literature. [1. Air pilots. 2. Aeronautics—Vocational guidance. 3. Vocational guidance.] I. Title.
TL547.A97 1990
629.13'0922—dc20   89-13488
                                     CIP
                                     AC

Manufactured in the United States of America

1 2 3 4 5 6 7 8 9 10 99 98 97 96 95 94 93 92 91 90

CONTENTS

Flying lessons begin here.

INTRODUCTION

Morey Airport is situated in a beautiful green field bordered by rolling hills of forest and farmland near Madison, Wisconsin. Here, around 9:30 on a Saturday morning, small airplanes sit quietly on the grass. Behind them are the offices of the Morey Airplane Company, where you have been taking flying lessons.

The wind sock barely ripples as a breeze stirs it from time to time. You check the local weather report and walk out to conduct a careful preflight check of your airplane. When your instructor arrives, you begin to practice **short-field takeoffs and landings**. You feel a sense of nervous excitement—you may solo (fly alone) for the first time today.

Back on the grass bordering the asphalt runway, your friends and family have spread a blanket. They have brought a cooler full of drinks and sandwiches; they're watching you practice. After your third landing, they notice that the aircraft has come to a full stop in the middle of the runway. There's a conversation going on in the cockpit.

Pretty soon, the airplane door opens and two legs appear. They hang there for a moment and then drop down to the asphalt. The door closes, and your family's munching stops. The instructor is walking away across the grass. Now it's *your* airplane.

You turn around and slowly **taxi** back down the runway, checking the sky for other airplanes that may be preparing to land. You line your aircraft up with the centerline of the runway, using your feet to steer. With your right hand, you advance the **throttle** that controls the airplane's engine.

There's a flutter as you lift off and depart upwind across the new corn. You make a shallow, 90-degree left turn and head crosswind, toward Madison's lakes. You make one more left turn, and you are at 800 feet (240 meters) and heading downwind for your first solo landing.

Solo flight in a single-engine airplane

As you fly past the numbers on the approach end of the runway, you begin to pull the throttle back to decrease your power. Your **airspeed** drops to 80 miles per hour (128 kilometers per hour). You lower your **flaps** 10 degrees just before turning left onto your **base leg.** You throttle back further and your airspeed continues to drop. Now that you have set your flaps at 30 degrees down, you are descending more slowly and steeply toward the runway.

As you turn left one more time, you line up your airplane with the runway centerline. Approaching at 60 miles an hour (96 km/h), you can see that you will touch down just beyond the numbers on the runway. You bring the airplane's nose up by pulling back on the **control yoke**—now hold it there—and you're down. The airplane rolls past the friends and family, and they whoop with delight. You make a 180-degree turn, taxi back, and grin. This feels good. You check for other airplanes that may be landing behind you, turn into the wind, and get ready to do it again.

Your family and friends go back to eating and talking. Your instructor is back at the office planning your next lesson. You are airborne again—you are becoming a pilot.

A new pilot scans the skies.

THE STUDENT PILOT

Student pilots want to fly more than anything else. They often dream of leaving home, school, or work behind and flying quickly and easily across the sky. Pilots have the freedom to travel all around the country, and they enjoy getting there as much as being there.

Beginning Flight Lessons

If you want to learn to fly, you can start taking lessons at a flight school like the Morey Airplane Company. Your first airplane will be a single-engine trainer like the Cessna 152. Trainers fly more slowly than most other airplanes and are very stable. They are designed to be forgiving of the mistakes that student pilots make. Flight lessons in a two-seat trainer with an instructor can cost about $50 an hour, so most student pilots find it necessary to have at least a part-time job to earn money for lessons. When you are ready for solo flight, your expenses will be less, since

A student pilot learns to use the rudder and control yoke to turn the airplane (opposite). Pilots must also perform weight-and-balance calculations that are essential to safe flight (above).

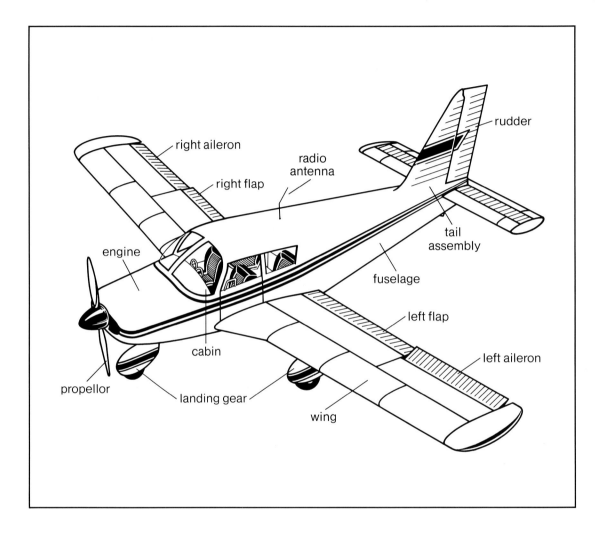

right aileron

radio antenna

right flap

rudder

engine

tail assembly

fuselage

cabin

left flap

left aileron

propellor

landing gear

wing

your only cost will be for the aircraft rental. At most flight schools, you can take lessons at your own pace and do a lot of the required studying at home.

During your first flight lesson, your instructor conducts a preflight check of the entire airplane—from the **propellor** up front to the **rudder** in back. The preflight check ensures that the engine, instruments, and controls will all work well once you are airborne. For example, your instructor drains some fuel from tanks in the airplane's wings to check for water and dirt. This ensures that the fuel is clean and will flow easily to the engine. Your instructor also checks a small device on the wing called a **pitot tube**. The pitot measures the pressure created by the airplane's forward movement through the air. The instructor makes sure that the tube is clear of insects and dirt. This ensures that the rate at which the air rushes past the airplane will be measured accurately, and, as a result, that your **airspeed indicator** will display the correct airspeed. You must know your airspeed to navigate and to fly safely.

Taxiing, or slowly moving the airplane to and from the runway, is nothing like driving a car. You steer the airplane with your feet by using two rudder pedals. You adjust the engine's power with a handheld throttle. If you are flying at a large airport with a **control tower**, such as Madison's Truax Field, your instructor asks for permission from **air traffic control** to taxi the airplane to the active runway—the one that's being used. The controller indicates what taxiways to follow to get to

the runway and notifies your instructor of the wind speed and direction.

Just before takeoff, your instructor turns the airplane into the wind, sets the brakes, and checks the flight instruments. He or she adjusts the **altimeter** so that it reads the airplane's **altitude**, or height above sea level, correctly. The instructor then pushes the throttle forward and checks that the engine is working well. If you are at a small airport without a control tower, your instructor scans the sky for incoming aircraft, turns onto the runway, and takes off. If you are at a large airport like Truax Field, he or she radios the air traffic controller in the tower and requests permission to take off. As you and your instructor **climb** out together, you head for a practice area a few miles away, where you begin your **air work**.

During your first lesson, your instructor helps you experience the feel of an airplane in flight. He or she teaches you to fly straight and level with the control yoke in one hand and the throttle in the other. Next you learn to turn. You use the control yoke to bank, or tip, your wings to one side or the other. Then you pull back a little on the control yoke and press your foot against the right or left rudder pedal. Done together, these actions turn the airplane.

When you first try using your hands and feet together in this way, you will have to concentrate hard. It takes practice to coordinate your hand and foot movements so that you can turn easily in any direction. The movable surfaces that actually turn the aircraft—the **ailerons** that bank the wings, the **elevators** that pitch the nose up or down, and the rudder that turns the airplane to the left or right—are all connected to the control yoke and the rudder pedals. As you learn to turn, you soon develop a feel for the airplane as a whole. You will be in full control as you guide your airplane from the pilot-in-command's left seat.

Learning How It's Done

As you learn to master turns, you also learn how to use the throttle to increase power for climbing and reduce power for **gliding** (decreasing your altitude). Wing flaps are attached to the rear, or trailing edge, of each wing. You soon learn that lowering your flaps (to a 30- or 40-degree angle, for instance) shortens your glide, or descent, without increasing your airspeed. This lets you get down and on the ground quickly when landing.

Finally, you learn to slow your airplane down so much that it **stalls**, or quits flying. You deliberately stall the aircraft so that you can learn how to regain airspeed if you slow down too much and accidentally stall during a climb, glide, or turn. Deliberate stalls may also help when landing. If you raise the aircraft's nose and stall the airplane just before touching down, you can gently lower your wheels onto the runway as you slow down.

Each student pilot is different, and each has a different level of ability. For some students, coordinating the controls when doing air work may come easily. In fact, turns, climbs, glides, **slow flight**, and stalls may all seem easy to do at 3,000 feet (900 m). At that altitude, the only objects the pilot must avoid are TV towers and other airplanes. Landings, however, tend to make student pilots sharpen their control skills, since pilots must accurately line up with the active runway and safely avoid trees and buildings during final approach.

A 172 Skyhawk (above). The cockpit of a Cessna 152 trainer (right). It takes many hours of air work and home study for a student pilot to master all the instruments and controls in the trainer.

Your First Solo

If you are at least 16 years old and have had about 15 to 20 hours of flight lessons, your instructor may decide to let you fly alone, or solo. He or she picks a day when the wind is calm. After half an hour of **dual instruction**, your instructor leaves you to fly the airplane alone. You take off, fly the standard rectangular **traffic pattern** around the airport, and return to land at the active runway. You may do that several times.

For most pilots, the first solo flight gives a genuine sense of accomplishment. Soloing represents that all-important first step toward becoming a pilot of any kind—including a private, commercial, or airline transport pilot. If you solo during high school, you have begun your flying career at the earliest and best possible time.

During solo flight, the student pilot receives instruction via her communication radio.

Flying lessons are demanding, but the freedom and excitement of flight make all the hard work worthwhile.

When you first dream of taking flying lessons, you may think that you will adapt naturally to your new wings. However, student pilots usually learn that even people who love flying for business or pleasure are not always "born to fly." Instead, they have learned to fly by making mistakes. Taking flight lessons can be hard work at first. With effort and persistence, you can learn the basic skills that all student pilots must have before they can leave their instructors and their home airports behind.

THE PRIVATE PILOT

You must log (pilots record all their flying time in a book called a flight log) at least 40 hours of dual instruction and solo flying time before you can take a flight test and a written exam to qualify for your private pilot's license. Once you have your private license, you can invite family members and friends aboard. As a private pilot, you can sharpen your skills in the Cessna 152 until you feel ready to have your instructor check you out in the larger and faster 172 Skyhawk or 182 Skylane. With a private license, you can fly for sheer enjoyment. You may enjoy camping and fishing trips, family trips to visit friends and relatives, and local flights within 30 miles (48 km) of your home base.

Even experienced pilots must inspect their aircraft prior to each flight (opposite). A special computer gives weather reports from reporting stations across the country (above).

Learning New Skills

Before you can receive a private license, however, you must continue your training as a student pilot. Using books and videotapes at home or at the airport, you need to learn important information about weather, navigation, and aircraft performance. Before each flight, you can get the latest weather reports from an airport computer that receives information from a weather satellite. You learn to read coded symbols on the computer's weather maps and printouts, which tell you the speed and direction of winds on the ground and aloft. The maps also show you if the weather is good, fair, or poor at airports all across the country and identify the clouds, rain, ice, and rough air that may affect your flight.

In the air, you learn to navigate with a special map for pilots called a **sectional chart**. There are symbols on the chart that tell you the location of landmarks like hills, TV towers, rivers, railway tracks, towns, and airports. By understanding the symbols on the chart, you can look out your window and find out where you are. In addition, you learn to use a hand-held **flight computer** to predict your **ground speed**. Ground speed, the speed at which your airplane travels over the earth, is different from airspeed. While your airspeed indicator measures the

airplane's speed through the air, it does not take into account tailwinds and headwinds that can decrease or increase your flying time. Ground speed calculations give you a more accurate measure of your estimated time of arrival (ETA) at your destination.

Your cross-country flight—flight from one airport to another—will become more precise once you learn to navigate by radio signals sent out by a radio station called a **VOR**. VOR stations (*v*ery high frequency *o*mnidirectional *r*ange stations) are also shown on sectional charts. You can fly from one airport to another by drawing your course line from airport #1 *to* the VOR on your route, and then *from* the VOR to airport #2.

If the first course you have drawn on your chart is due east (90 degrees on the magnetic compass), you turn your airplane to fly east toward the VOR station. To make sure you are flying precisely to the station, you tune your **navigation radio** to the VOR's **frequency** and turn your **radio course** selector to 90 degrees. If you are directly on your 90-degree course toward the station, the needle on the **TO-FROM indicator** on your instrument panel will be centered. The TO-FROM indicator will also read "TO," showing that you are flying *toward* the station. You adjust your airplane's direction as necessary to keep the needle centered and stay precisely on course.

Once you have flown past the VOR station, the TO-FROM indicator will read "FROM." If you need to fly southeast (135 degrees on the magnetic compass) to reach airport #2, you select 135 degrees on your radio course selector. You turn your airplane until you are flying southeast and the compass on your instrument panel shows 135 degrees. If you are flying accurately along the 135-degree course away from the VOR station, the needle on the TO-FROM indicator will be centered once again.

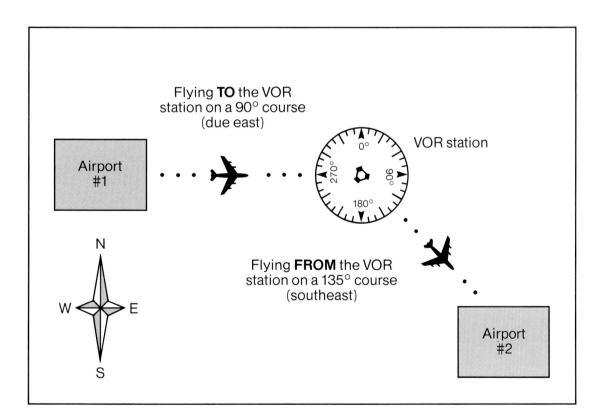

As you fly along each course, you may notice landmarks such as towns and rivers. By flying the course accurately (keeping the needle centered on the TO-FROM indicator) and watching for landmarks, you can locate your position on the sectional chart.

As you continue along the course, you eventually see your destination airport. As you get closer and closer, you will be able to see the runways. Now you can turn off your navigation radio and call the control tower with your **communication radio** for landing instructions. In this way, you can fly from one airport to another by using your eyes, your radios, and your sectional chart.

Before any flight, the pilot uses a hand-held aviation computer to compute ground speed, weight-and-balance limits, and fuel requirements. The pilot also maps out his or her route on a sectional chart (background).

Flying in Unexpected Situations

Before you soloed, you only knew how to land in gentle winds that were blowing straight along the runway, or close to it. Now you must learn to land safely when the wind direction has shifted to the right or left, and perhaps picked up speed. You learn how to hold one wing a little lower than the other and how to turn your airplane's nose a few degrees into the wind during the final approach. Both methods will keep you flying right along the center-line of the runway in crosswinds and gusty conditions.

As you continue to study and fly with your instructor, you learn some skills that may help you in unusual situations or emergencies. For example, by keeping two "wings" level with a "horizon line" on a flight instrument called an **attitude indicator**, you can keep your airplane's wings level with the horizon without looking out of the window. If you were returning home and an overcast sky closed in underneath you, the attitude indicator would help you keep your wings level as you descended into the clouds and lost sight of the ground.

The attitude indicator has a "nose" and two "wings" that show the pilot whether the airplane is level with the horizon. The indicator above shows that the airplane is in a shallow climbing turn to the left.

Solo cross-country flight in a Cessna 152

One day, perhaps on a cross-country flight with your instructor, you may be surprised when he or she calmly reduces power by pulling the throttle all the way back. Your instructor does this to teach you how to set up an approach toward a road or field where you can make a safe landing in the rare event of an engine failure. Once you are successfully approaching your chosen landing spot, your instructor can quickly and easily restore full engine power by pushing the throttle forward again.

Becoming a Private Pilot

As a student pilot, your instructor judges your skills at every level in the private pilot training program. To become a licensed private pilot, you also have to show a flight examiner from the Federal Aviation Administration (FAA) that you know what you are doing in the air and on the ground. The FAA is a branch of the federal government that sets the rules and safety standards under which pilots fly in the United States.

During your flight test, the FAA examiner's job is to judge whether you can fly smoothly, accurately, and with judgment—in short, whether you are in control of the aircraft at all times. "Thinking ahead of the airplane"—knowing what is needed ahead of time—is a flying skill that is important for the safety and success of any flight. Also important is "flying within your capabilities"—flying only in weather and in airplanes that you can safely handle alone.

Flying safely in a small airplane requires knowledge, experience, and judgment. For this reason, flight instructors say that the private pilot's license is really a license to learn.

A student pilot and an FAA examiner. To earn his private pilot's license, the student must pass a written and a flight exam.

THE INSTRUMENT RATING

With the aid of communication and navigation radios (top right), instrument-rated pilots fly to and from VOR stations. The TO-FROM indicator is at top left.

Once you have earned your private pilot's license, you will be able to fly locally and cross-country for personal enjoyment. The more you fly, the more you will learn about the art of flying. One good way to develop your new flying skill is to begin working toward your FAA **instrument rating**. A private pilot who has earned his or her instrument rating is able to fly by referring only to the aircraft's instruments and radios when the weather is poor.

An instrument-rated private pilot is capable of navigating cross-country when visibility is poor, and low clouds and bad weather are keeping non-rated pilots on the ground. Pilots who earn their instrument ratings increase the usefulness of their airplanes, since they can use them safely and efficiently when the weather is poor.

Pilots flying under visual flight rules (VFR) must stay well clear of clouds. They must also stay on the ground if visibility is less than three miles.

The private pilot flying by **visual flight rules (VFR)** can only fly when the weather is fair to good, or above **"VFR minimums."** These rules, set by the FAA, say that VFR-rated pilots may take off and land only if the cloud ceiling is greater than 1,000 feet (300 m) and visibility (the distance pilots can see clearly) is over 3 miles (4.8 km). The experienced instrument-rated pilot, on the other hand, may fly through clouds and when visibility is well under three miles. The FAA's **instrument flight rules (IFR)** govern flight procedures when the weather is fair to poor, or below VFR minimums.

There are limits that instrument-rated pilots must respect, however. First, they must stay away from thunderstorms; the violent air currents within these storms can tear a small airplane to shreds. Second, pilots must avoid "icing conditions." A buildup of ice on the outside of an airplane can increase the aircraft's weight beyond safe limits and change the shape of its wings— decreasing the wings' ability to keep the airplane aloft.

Learning to Fly IFR

As a private pilot learning to fly by instrument flight rules, you wear a special hood that allows you to see only the instruments on the panel in front of you. The hood prevents you from seeing out the airplane's windows, just the way clouds and rain would if you were flying in poor weather.

As you fly, your instructor keeps an eye on the air traffic around you and asks you to fly from one point to another by referring to your instruments alone. In this way, the instructor plays the role of the air traffic controllers who will guide you during actual instrument flights. Your instructor may also ask you to make climbing and descending turns as practice for making instrument-guided departures from and approaches to the active runway.

When learning to fly under instrument flight rules, you must fly in an airplane that has some special kinds of instruments and radios. While flying under the hood, you refer regularly to your attitude indicator. The attitude indicator lets you turn safely and keep your wings level when you cannot see the ground.

In addition, you use navigation radios, which make travel along VOR radio courses possible, and communication radios, which allow you to talk to air traffic controllers. During actual IFR flight, the controllers tell you when and where to fly as you depart from your home base, cruise on course, and approach your destination.

Air traffic controllers monitor and direct the movement of aircraft on instrument flight plans from takeoff through touchdown.

Preparing to Fly IFR

When preparing to make a cross-country trip by instrument flight rules, you first need to learn about the weather along the route to your destination. You may receive this information from an airport weather computer, or you may call a flight service station by phone and discuss the weather with an FAA specialist. There are flight service stations in each state, and the specialists who staff them assist all pilots with flight planning.

The specialist you contact describes the weather all along your route. He or she gives you the weather conditions at the time of your call and tells you the forecast for the next several hours. Knowing the forecast weather along your route helps you decide whether to take off as planned or stay on the ground. Your decision to go or stay depends on the severity of the weather, how much instrument flying experience you have logged, and your honest assessment of your own flying skills.

IFR skills are especially important at night, when pilots can't rely on their eyes for navigation.

Once you have decided to take off, the flight service specialist will need your IFR flight plan. Your flight plan tells the specialist which airport you are departing from, what route and altitude you want to fly, and where you want to land. The plan also lists an alternate airport where you will land if weather conditions at your destination become dangerous. After the specialist has recorded all the information on a flight planning card, he or she alerts air traffic control of your flight plan by phone. An air traffic controller will start to follow your flight on a **radar** screen when you make radio contact with the first control tower along your route, shortly after takeoff.

Flying IFR

As you leave your home airport behind, a departure controller tells you which **headings** to fly to stay on course and reach your destination. A heading is simply a direction, corresponding to the magnetic compass, in which 0 degrees indicates due north and 180 degrees indicates due south. You find your heading by turning your airplane until your compass reads the

The gyro compass shows the pilot exactly which way the aircraft is headed.

heading you have been assigned. Once you are 25 to 30 miles (40 to 50 km) outbound, the departure controller instructs you to contact an en route air traffic control center, which will monitor your progress as you cruise toward your destination.

Controllers in the en route traffic control center watch your progress on a radar screen as you fly along the radio courses listed on your flight plan. You turn your navigation radio to the frequency of the first VOR station on your route and select the radio course that will take you toward the station.

The radios—essential tools for navigation and for communication with air traffic control during IFR flight. This pilot's communication radio is tuned to air traffic control on a frequency of 124. The navigation radio is tuned to a VOR station on a frequency of 108.60.

The needle on your TO-FROM indicator centers itself when you are flying directly along the course you have selected. If the needle moves to the left or right, you must change your heading a few degrees until the needle is centered again.

As you can see, radio skills become very important for the pilot flying by instrument flight rules. Whenever an en route controller gives you instructions to fly a certain heading, radio course, or altitude, you must repeat his or her instructions. In this way, the controller knows that you understand exactly what to do next. The same is true when you receive instructions from a departure controller after takeoff, or from an approach controller before you land.

As you approach your destination, you may use a VOR station at or near the airport to give you radio guidance until you can see the runway in front of you. When clouds are low, however, you may need to make a "precision approach" down to the runway. You do this by tuning your navigation radio to the **instrument landing system (ILS)** frequency and keeping your TO-FROM needle centered once again.

The ILS radio signals, which are transmitted from an antenna next to the runway, help you line up with the runway until you break out of the clouds. If you still cannot see the runway when you are 200 feet (60 m) above the airport surface, you may fly back around and try again or go to an alternate airport where visibility is better.

Keeping Your Head out of the Clouds

The newly-rated instrument pilot should avoid weather that requires him or her to fly for long periods in the clouds. The best policy is to use instrument flight procedures to get *above* fog and low clouds and to fly in clear air, rather than taking off into weather that will keep you in clouds for most of the flight.

As you gain experience flying in IFR weather conditions, you may go on personal, family, and business trips without having to wait for the weather to clear. You have to avoid becoming careless or overconfident, however. As a careful and well-prepared pilot, you will know that your private pilot's license, even with an instrument rating, is still a license to learn.

AIR TRAFFIC CONTROL

FAA controllers who operate the air traffic control system in the United States must provide safe distances around, above, and below each aircraft. Their work ensures that the flow of air traffic across the country is as safe and efficient as possible. Controllers also decide whether pilots may fly by visual flight rules, or whether clouds and poor visibility make instrument flight rules necessary for the safety of pilots and their passengers.

Local and Ground Control

Local controllers guide aircraft around the airport's traffic pattern during takeoffs and landings. The traffic pattern is a rectangular flight path that extends from the runway up to 800 feet (240 m) above ground level. It is made up of four legs: upwind (into the wind),

A controller watches aircraft movement on radar (opposite). The tower at Truax Field gives controllers a good view of aircraft on the ground and in the air (above).

crosswind, downwind (with the wind), and base. Local controllers manage traffic within this pattern, while ground controllers manage traffic on the airport's taxiways and parking ramps.

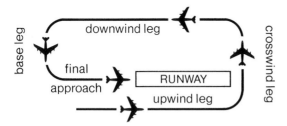

Departure and Approach Control

Working in a radar room near the control tower, approach and departure controllers monitor the progress of airplanes within about 30 miles (48 km) of the airport. The controllers watch the aircraft on radar screens, making sure there is adequate distance all around each airplane and guiding pilots safely to their proper altitudes and courses.

A ground controller surveys the traffic at Truax Field.

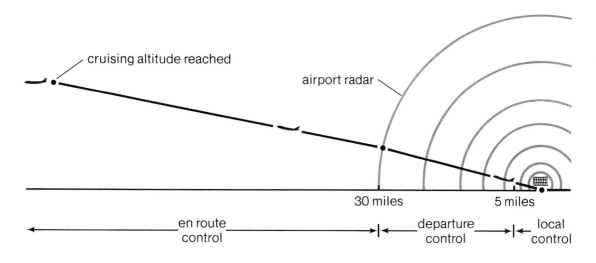

The airplane passes from local to departure to en route control as it climbs to its cruising course and altitude.

Air Traffic Control During IFR Flight

Once a flight service station takes your flight plan, you receive clearance by telephone (at an airport that doesn't have a control tower) or by radio (at a controlled airport) to depart. After take-off, the departure controller watches your aircraft on his or her radar screen and guides you around other aircraft as you climb toward your proper radio course and cruising altitude.

As you continue to climb toward cruising altitude, responsibility for monitoring your progress passes from departure control to an en route air traffic control center. By watching their radar screens and staying in radio contact with you, center controllers along your route help to ensure your safe and accurate navigation throughout your flight.

As you fly toward your destination, you may tune in an **automatic terminal information service (ATIS)** that is broadcast from many control towers. The recorded voice of a tower controller will give you the current weather at your destination, the active runway, and the radio frequencies you need for approach, local, and ground control. This service gives you time to plan your approach and prepare for the weather conditions you will encounter during your descent.

After the en route controller tells you to begin your descent, you switch your radio to the approach controller's frequency. The approach controller continues to give you headings until you are on your final approach to the active runway. There, a few miles from the airport, you change your radio frequency again and contact the local controller for clearance to land.

Air Traffic Control and VFR Flight

Pilots flying VFR may also use air traffic control services. If you are flying VFR on a hazy day, for example, you might ask an approach controller for **vectors**, or headings, to the active runway if you cannot see it. Pilots flying VFR into controlled airports must contact local controllers for clearance to taxi to the active runway, take off, and land. Even so, they must guide themselves visually around the traffic pattern when flying away from or back to the runway. Air traffic controllers are also ready to help VFR pilots who have an in-flight emergency.

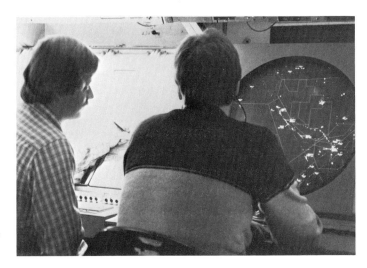

Controllers at the Los Angeles Air Route Traffic Control Center.

Uncontrolled Airports

Uncontrolled airports have the same traffic pattern as controlled airports. But rather than ask for clearance to taxi, take off, and land, pilots at uncontrolled airports announce their intentions over the airport's **unicom** frequency. A unicom is an airport radio station that provides pilots with local information about wind speed and direction, altimeter setting, and the runway in use. You are not required to use the unicom frequency, but it is helpful to others flying nearby when you announce your position and intentions in the traffic pattern.

Please Ask

FAA air traffic controllers do a very important job as they clear pilots to progress from one point to the next. In addition, they provide life-saving assistance to pilots with limited experience who have an in-flight emergency. If you become disoriented by increasing clouds or reduced visibility during a flight, ask for help. For you—and for all pilots—expert guidance to a safe landing is just a radio call away.

Communication with air traffic controllers is essential for safety at large airports. At small, uncontrolled airports, pilots must look out for themselves and others.

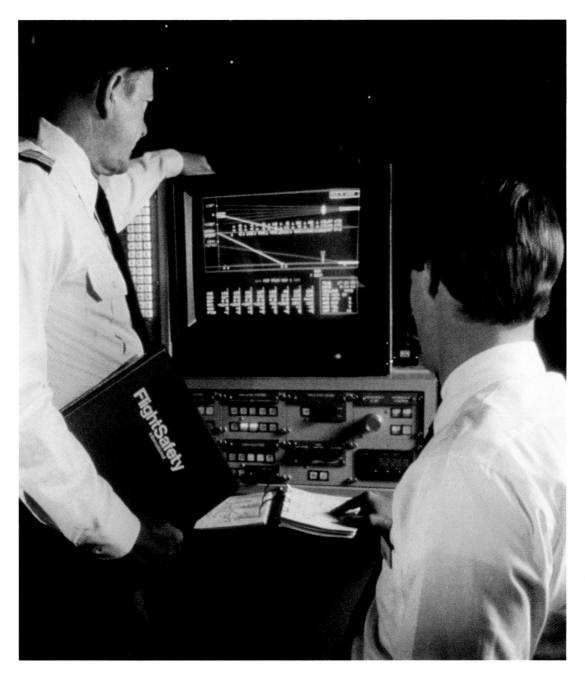

YOUR CAREER
IN AVIATION

Aviation is a growing industry in need of highly skilled pilots. Some pilots want to fly for the military (above). A pilot who wants to work for the major airlines must log thousands of hours of flight time and receive advanced training (opposite).

It is never too early to begin thinking about an aviation career. If you are in your teens, you can start working now toward an airline captain's job. You can learn to solo in a sailplane (an engineless airplane) at age 14 and in a powered airplane when you are 16. You can get your private license at age 17 and your commercial license when you are 18. You can also spend time at the airport before and after lessons and listen to other pilots talk about weather, navigation, and their recent flight experiences.

If you are in junior high or high school, learning to fly will give you a "real world" goal to work toward. As your involvement in flying grows, schoolwork will become more important. Your school counselor can assign you to math, English, and science courses that will prepare you for a college level aviation program. Unlike many other students in school, you will know where you want to go with your life. You will be preparing to enter a dynamic industry that offers young people the chance to become as fully involved as they want to be.

The Future of Aviation

Aviation is projected to be a "growth industry" up to and beyond the year 2000. In this sense, aviation means more than studying weather and navigating airplanes cross-country. Aviation refers to a profession in which thousands of people do many different kinds of work that together make flying airplanes a successful and profitable enterprise. The aviation industry needs airport managers, air traffic controllers, mechanics, and avionic (aviation electronics) technicians, as well as pilots. The industry will also need as many as 4,000 new aircraft by the year 2000 to meet the needs of commuter, regional, and major airlines.

The airlines have a lot to offer pilots who want an aviation career. In recent years, airlines have been scheduling more and more flights. As a result, there has been an ever-increasing need for good airline pilots. The airlines want to hire highly motivated and experienced pilots and help them to develop their flying skills to the fullest.

Academics Are Important

To prepare for a career in aviation, it is important to look for a college or university with an aviation program. There is no standard process by which pilots are trained for an airline career. The best route to a career in aviation is through advanced flight training and a degree in **airway science**. Colleges and universities that emphasize communications, psychology, and business administration, as well as math, physics, and computer science, provide the best education for a career pilot.

By pairing the arts and sciences with a comprehensive **ground school** and flight training program, you can prepare to become an airline executive as well as an airline pilot. You can also receive high-quality training at an airport near your home, college, or university. From there, you can gain experience as a flight instructor, charter pilot, freight pilot, commuter airline pilot, or corporate pilot.

The cockpit can become "the office" for those who want a flying career.

Enthusiasm Is Everything

All pilots hired by the major airlines have one thing in common: they have an intense commitment to flying. A pilot has to give up time with family and friends to build time and experience in the cockpit. Flying charters and giving flight lessons pay far less than does working as an airline captain. These jobs require pilots to work long hours at inconvenient times of the day or night. It is time well spent, however, because these positions give you the experience that you will need when you occupy the captain's seat in a jumbo jet cockpit.

THE COMMERCIAL PILOT

The commercial license allows pilots to fly for hire and gives them many job options. Commercial pilots fly charters, give sight-seeing tours, spray crops, operate air ambulance services, work as test pilots, and more.

One sure way to increase your knowledge and professionalism in the cockpit is to get your commercial pilot's license. Even private pilots who have no interest in flying for hire may choose to get their "commercial tickets" because the training they receive improves the quality and safety of their flight operations. Much of the commercial pilot curriculum is a review of the private and instrument pilot's knowledge and skills, and a presentation of new information about weather, navigation, high-performance aircraft, and efficient flight planning.

You will first become familiar with commercial aviation while watching your flight instructor at work during your lessons. To be able to carry paying passengers or teach others to fly, your instructor has had to earn a commercial license. What you may not realize is that you yourself are working toward your

45

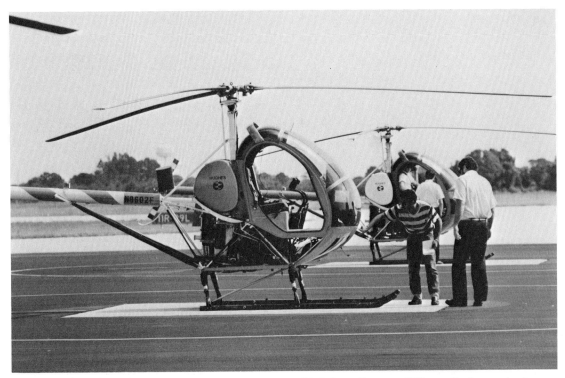

Commercial pilots may learn to fly helicopters, which handle very differently from airplanes.

commercial license every time you receive instruction and log flight time as a student, private, or instrument-rated pilot. You will need 250 hours or more of flight time, including more dual instruction, to qualify for your commercial license. By the time you complete the training and pass the written and flight tests, your skills will have increased significantly.

Precise Flying

To earn your commercial license, you will need more instruction. You will develop your ability to use the throttle, control yoke, and rudder pedals together, until you feel (and your instructor observes) a definite increase in your ability to control the airplane under all flight conditions. To accomplish this, your instructor has you fly figure-eight patterns around two objects on the ground. By changing the steepness of the turn at various points around the figure eight, you learn to compensate for the effects of the wind's speed and direction on your airplane. This gives you a better sense of how to control your aircraft with precision when you are flying in unexpected or difficult situations.

Respecting Limitations

Operating an airplane within its limitations is basic to safe flight. During your commercial training, your instructor reviews passenger and cargo loading. When preparing to carry a full load of passengers and baggage, you use the weight-and-balance tables in your airplane's operating handbook to make sure that your aircraft will be neither overloaded nor tailheavy. Overloaded airplanes do not fly safely or predictably. Tailheavy airplanes may stall shortly after takeoff and spin into the ground.

Understanding and preparing for the effects of water vapor and air temperature on aircraft performance is just as important as learning how to load your aircraft correctly. On a cold, dry day in winter, your engine has more power and your wings provide more **lift** than they do on a hot, humid

Preflight planning becomes more complex for the commercial pilot who carries a full load of passengers and baggage.

A twin-engine airplane. A commercial pilot will eventually take the airline transport pilot flight exam in a light twin like this.

summer day. Because you have less power during the summer, you will need a longer runway to build up enough speed and lift to become airborne. To calculate the length of the runway needed for takeoff, you use your flight computer and additional tables located in your aircraft's operating handbook. If you need more runway than is available at your airport, you either have to lighten your airplane or stay on the ground.

Greater Efficiency

It is important for commercial pilots to feel confident that they can conduct their flight operations safely whenever they are asked to fly. To this end, your commercial training includes a review of how, when, and why to contact air traffic controllers when flying IFR or VFR into busy airports, and how to land and take off safely from rural airports with short, grass runways. Your instructor may also show you special publications that are useful for pilots when they fly cross-country. These publications enable you to learn more about your destination airports and to conduct your cross-country flights with more safety and efficiency.

As a private pilot, you log many hours flying cross-country in airplanes like the Cessna 152 and the 172 Skyhawk. As you continue to develop your cross-country flight skills, your instructor will introduce you to faster and more complex aircraft such as the 182 Skylane RG or the 210 Centurion. Both are high-performance airplanes with additional capabilities and controls, such as adjustable-pitch propellors and retractable landing gear. When flying these aircraft, your instructor shows you how to increase your speed by adjusting the angle of your propellor blades during flight. Your instructor also shows you how to raise the airplane's landing gear to increase airspeed after takeoff, and how to lower the gear to reduce airspeed prior to landing.

Flying for Hire

The commercial pilot's license, the first FAA license that permits you to fly for hire, lets you participate in the world of aviation much more fully than does your private license. Commercial pilots work as flight instructors and charter pilots at airports around the country.

At Morey Airport, for example, flight instructor Scott Capener spends 25 percent of his time flying charters (cross-country flights arranged for small groups of people) and 75 percent of his time teaching private, instrument, commercial, and multiengine flight. For charters, Scott flies the Cessna 340 to transport regular customers such as engineers, doctors, company executives, lawyers, and construction teams to various points within a 500-mile (800-km) radius of the airport.

Flight instructors must have a commercial license.

Your Multiengine Rating

A commercial pilot who provides both flight instruction and charter service will need to earn a multiengine rating. A multiengine rating allows a pilot to fly the twin-engine aircraft often used for charter flights. Just as important, multiengine flight experience puts a pilot within closer reach of a career flying for the major airlines.

Flying a twin-engine airplane is similar to flying a single-engine airplane in many respects, but there are some new and important skills to learn. For example, when flying in a twin-engine airplane, you need to know how to keep control of the airplane should you lose one engine. During multiengine flight instruction, you learn how to use your rudder pedals and power from the good engine to keep flying on course, even if one engine fails.

Teaching and More

You also need additional ground and flight instruction to become a certified flight instructor (CFI). The additional training focuses primarily on how to work with people. This is important because an instructor needs to judge when a student has the confidence and skills to fly solo "around the patch" (around the airport's traffic pattern) and cross-country. In addition, there are times when a flight instructor needs to provide gentle guidance to a student or private pilot who is preparing for a flight which, for him or her, might be difficult or even dangerous. Typically, instructors are calm, stable people who instill confidence in their students and are sensitive to each student's skills, abilities, and needs.

Commercial pilots might fly charters or carry cargo and mail in this Cessna Caravan I.

In addition to instructional and charter flying, commercial pilots give sight-seeing tours, spray crops with fertilizer and insecticide, do aerial advertising and photography, fly cargo and mail nationwide, and operate air ambulance services. They also work for aircraft companies as test pilots and evaluate the flight characteristics of new aircraft.

Compared to private pilots, commercial pilots are more knowledgeable and skillful in the preparation and execution of their flight plans. As a commercial pilot, you refine your skills so that your flying is much more precise. As you gain flight time and experience, you may qualify for a position as a first officer (copilot) with a commuter airline.

THE AIRLINE TRANSPORT PILOT

Flying an approach in a computer-driven flight simulator (opposite). A commuter airline pilot (above).

A pilot who wants to fly for a major airline must have an airline transport pilot's license (ATP). When hiring new pilots, the major airlines look for candidates with the ATP certificate and lots of flight experience.

Commuter Aviation

While many pilots want to fly for a major airline, there are other airline careers that are challenging and rewarding. Pilots with a commercial license can get their first experience with a scheduled airline by flying commuter airplanes. Commuter pilots fly groups of people from small airports that aren't serviced by the major airlines to large airports, usually near a large city.

As a commuter airline pilot, you often have to fly an entire day "by hand"—without an **autopilot** to keep the airplane on the correct

The Cessna 402 Businessliner

course and altitude. Because you fly over relatively short distances, your descent may begin after only a brief time at cruising altitude. Your work continually changes as you move from taxi to takeoff, climb to cruise, and approach to landing. When on the ground, you are also responsible for everything from loading luggage and overseeing the refueling process to staying on schedule at stop after stop.

Corporate Aviation

Many U.S. corporations maintain a fleet of airplanes and fly their executives around the country. As a corporate pilot, you may transport business executives in high-performance jets, many of which have advanced radios and instrumentation, as well as propellor-driven aircraft. Like commuter airline pilots, corporate pilots are responsible for every aspect of the flight.

Unlike commuter airline pilots, corporate pilots fly anywhere their executive passengers want them to fly. As a corporate pilot you are not bound by a strict schedule. Even so, you still must attend to such jobs as planning refreshments and greeting passengers. When flying for a corporation, you are a manager who teams with other corporate managers to get the company's business done. Flights are not always repetitive or routine. As a corporate pilot, you may fly within a state or two, around the country, and even overseas when business requires it.

Corporate pilots fly business executives around the country and overseas. They are responsible for all aspects of the flight—loading luggage, fueling, preflight inspection, and greeting passengers.

The Major Airlines

There are also excellent career opportunities for pilots who want to continue their professional progress with a national or international airline. In addition to lifelong training, flying for "the majors" includes much higher pay and, as a pilot develops seniority, a choice of routes and schedules.

United Airlines currently employs 6,700 pilots. It carries an average of 155,000 passengers a day using a fleet of over 400 Boeing and McDonnell Douglas jet transports.

Because successful applicants to the major airlines have flown for many years with commuter and regional airlines or with the military, they tend to be approaching middle age. At United Airlines, the average applicant for a pilot position is 33 years old. College graduates make up 70 percent

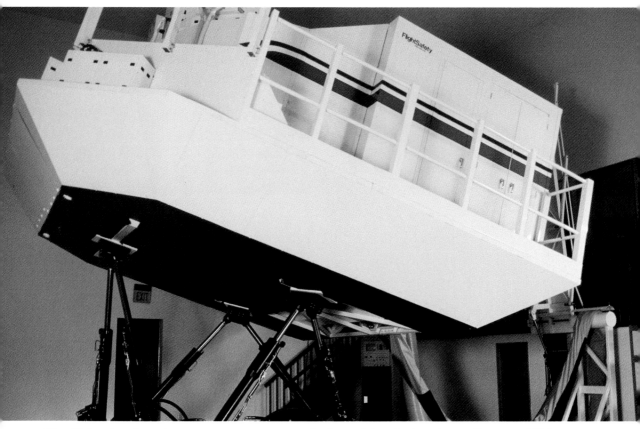

The flight simulator is an enormous computerized machine. It simulates all sorts of flight situations: takeoffs and landings, approaches, severe weather, instrument failure, engine fires—even crash landings. By training in the simulator, pilots perfect their skills with jet transports and learn to handle emergency situations.

of the applicants, while another 19 percent have completed some college course work. Most applicants have logged over 4,000 flight hours, and 90 percent have the ATP license.

Lifelong Training

The ATP flight exam is where your flying skills are tested much more stringently than they were during your private, instrument, commercial, and multiengine flight tests. For example, during your flight test, the FAA examiner may shut down one engine while you are flying an instrument approach with a hood on—and expect you to keep on flying the approach. The ability to handle this kind of situation smoothly comes only with extensive knowledge and experience. This is one reason why you must have logged at least 1,500 hours of flight time to qualify for the ATP.

When applying for a position with a major airline, you will be tested in **flight simulators** and interviewed at length to make sure that you are a qualified candidate for the airline's pilot training program. You begin your training upon acceptance and continue to train in classrooms and simulators throughout your airline flying career. Because you may be dropped from consideration at any point in the application process, you need to be motivated, clear-headed, and very well prepared.

Once hired, you undergo several weeks of ground school and six weeks of **flight engineer** training. At United's training center in Denver, Colorado, 500 technicians and teachers help train pilots at all stages of their careers. For new pilots, there is little time for anything except intense study and skill development.

Flight simulators are used during many of the training sessions. These machines help you get used to new equipment and flight procedures. Later on, you and your crew "fly" through simulated in-flight emergencies such as severe weather, instrument failure, engine fires, and even crash landings. By experiencing a variety of simulated flight conditions safely and repeatedly, you increase and maintain your knowledge and skills.

Encouraging Teamwork

In addition to the captain, airliners usually have a first officer, or copilot, and a second officer, or flight engineer, in the cockpit. The flight engineer position is usually filled by newly hired pilots. As a flight engineer, your primary responsibility is to ensure safe and efficient aircraft performance. During preflight, you check the airframe (the body of the aircraft), the airplane's electrical and mechanical systems, and the engines. You also oversee the fueling of the aircraft, while the captain

A 747 parked in a hangar at United Airline's Maintenance Operations Center in San Francisco. United's maintenance staff keeps over 400 jetliners in top condition.

and first officer study the weather at your departure, destination, and alternate airports.

Even more important than your individual work assignments, however, is your ability to work as a team with your captain and first officer. No single person can manage all the systems on a large airline jet alone. Without teamwork, the risk of an accident increases. Research has shown that most fatal aircraft accidents happen because crew members are not working together as a team.

To help their pilots fly as effective teams, United Airlines has developed seminars and home study materials to help each crew member build better leadership and problem-solving skills.

Cooperation in the Cockpit

Effective teamwork in the cockpit is the key to safe flight in any airplane. This is particularly true when flying multiengine jet airplanes. As the captain advances the throttle to full power for takeoff, the first officer calls out critical speeds as they are reached: the speed at which the captain must continue takeoff even if an engine fails, the speed at which the captain puts the airplane into a nose-up position, and the speed at which the airplane can leave the ground.

Once the flying pilots have established a climb toward cruising altitude, the flight engineer must watch over all the systems, such as cabin pressurization and fuel consumption, that affect the safety and comfort of both passengers and crew. As a flight engineer, you will have to keep refiguring your weight-and-balance calculations in flight. A jet engine burns off tons of fuel during a flight, so one section of the airplane can become much lighter than another. To keep the aircraft balanced, you must pump fuel from one tank to another. By managing all the mechanical systems within the airplane, you help the two flying pilots get the safest and best performance from the aircraft at each stage of the flight.

During approach and landing, you calculate the correct approach and landing speeds for the weight of your aircraft, which may have burned as much as 100 tons of fuel during the flight. Throughout the approach, the flying pilots fly very smoothly and carefully, correcting for any crosswind or turbulence as soon as it is detected. You, meanwhile, watch all the gauges on the instrument panels in the cockpit to ensure that no important information is overlooked. With this combined guidance, the airplane stays precisely on course as it comes in toward the runway with landing gear and wing flaps fully extended.

Professional Responsibility

There is no reason why private and commercial pilots cannot develop the discipline and precision of an airline crew. Your own flying abilities can be as safe and professional as you want to make them. Do your best to excel in your private flight lessons and your required high school coursework. As you progress personally and academically, you will be helping yourself succeed in the world of professional pilots and aviation.

THE FIGHTER PILOT

For pilots and non-pilots alike, the sight of jet fighters in flight can be downright awesome! No one flies fighters better than the Navy's Blue Angels and the Air Force's Thunderbirds. In F/A-18 Hornets and F-16 Fighting Falcons, these aerobatic teams play to crowds of thousands around the United States and the world. The aircraft are spectacular to watch as they maneuver in close formation. Fighter pilots love them, and they handle beautifully. In most cases, pilots enter military service specifically to fly fighters.

Four F-14A pilots fly in formation over their aircraft carrier, the U.S.S. Dwight D. Eisenhower (opposite). Women serve in non-combat roles in the military as flight instructors, transport pilots, and executive jet pilots.

Flying on the Edge

The fighter pilot's daily reality is different, however, from what people watch during an air show or see in a popular movie like *Top Gun*. Training for combat is exhausting. In a "dogfight," the aircraft is constantly changing directions. **Centrifugal forces** up to nine times that of gravity can crush you down into your seat. Blood will drain away from your brain as you fly your aircraft to the limits of your strength and intellect. You must find the fine line at which your aircraft performs with both the greatest speed and the greatest maneuverability. Being able to bring your fighter's flight performance to this edge—and maintain it—often means the difference between living and dying for the pilot in combat.

In simulated combat, you must be able to manage large quantities of information that all clamor for your attention. Jet-powered intruders in the sky around you, as well as computer displays in your own cockpit, will

A U.S. Navy fighter pilot prepares for takeoff in the F-4 Phantom.

A flight deck crew launches an F-18 Hornet over the Pacific Ocean.

require you to prioritize and respond to as many as eight tasks or situations every second. Once you detect an adversary in the sky, you must decide what to do and act in an instant. The intense concentration required throughout the mission can result in pilot fatigue and increased vulnerability to attack. To survive, the fighter pilot must make the right combination of flying and fighting moves in a constantly changing combat environment.

This pilot, 30,000 feet above the ocean in an F-14 Tomcat, can check his navigation and weapons information through the head-up display and still keep his eyes on other aircraft outside.

Carrier-Based Fighter Pilots

Some of the most demanding fighter flying occurs when naval aviators go to sea. As a Navy pilot on an aircraft carrier, you must always be ready for combat. Your work is demanding each and every time you fly. When flying a defensive mission, your primary job is to maintain mastery of the sky all around the aircraft carrier. Incoming hostile aircraft or missiles must be destroyed. When flying an attack mission, your primary responsibility is to destroy the enemy's airfields, troops, and supply lines.

When engaging an enemy aircraft, all the targeting and flight information you need will be found on the transparent **head-up display (HUD)** in front of you. Information normally shown on the instrument panel—airspeed, fuel consumption, altitude, and so on—is instead displayed on HUD, two glass plates just inside the airplane's windshield. By looking through the glass plates, you can see navigation and weapons systems information while keeping your eyes on hostile aircraft. When you return to the carrier enshrouded by rain, fog, or the blackness of night, the carrier's deck can be all but invisible. To land safely, split-second timing and total concentration are needed once again.

Thinking Ahead

Becoming a fighter pilot may seem exciting when you are watching the Blue Angels or Thunderbirds, but there is nothing easy or glorious about it. Many pilots who want to fly jet fighters fail the rigorous flight school curriculum or are assigned to flying military transport airplanes instead. For those who make it, the exhilaration of flying fighters is always tempered with the sober realities of military service Learning to fly and fight with high-tech, high-speed fighter aircraft requires that pilots stay calm under tremendous pressure. There are also daily administrative responsibilities for the fighter pilot that don't relate at all to flying.

The Navy and Air Force provide the toughest training and the toughest flying anywhere. Talk to someone who has been a fighter pilot—and then do some serious thinking—before pursuing a military flight career.

To land safely on the deck of an aircraft carrier, a pilot needs split-second timing and total concentration.

PILOTS FROM ALL OVER

The EAA Fly-In (opposite) brings hundreds of thousands of pilots to Oshkosh, Wisconsin, every August. The attendees include home-builders, student pilots, astronauts, and celebrities like Dick Rutan and Jeana Yeager (above), who flew nonstop around the world.

Every year pilots from all 50 states and over 70 countries around the world gather at Wittman Field, 90 miles (144 km) northeast of Madison in Oshkosh, Wisconsin. These pilots come to learn about some aspect of aviation that truly fascinates them. They also come just to look, listen, and experience the grandeur and excitement of aviation. Home to the world headquarters of the Experimental Aircraft Association (EAA), Wittman Field becomes the world's busiest airport around August first, when 15,000 aircraft make the trip to the EAA's annual Fly-In convention. For more than 750,000 pilots and non-pilots alike, the Fly-In embodies everything they love about aviation.

Everyone enjoys the afternoon air shows at the Fly-In.

Everyone Comes

The EAA was founded in 1953 by Paul and Audrey Poberezny and a small group of pilots to encourage home airplane building and sport aviation. Today, EAA chapters around the country and abroad provide support for individuals who are building a personal airplane. At the Fly-In, classes like "Composite Basics" (working with fiberglass) and "Flight-Testing Your Homebuilt" are offered for homebuilders at all stages of construction.

But the Fly-In isn't just for homebuilders. During the week-long event, the flight line—the line of parked airplanes—is full of people and aircraft of every kind. Pilots visiting the convention arrive in everything from ultralights to the supersonic Concorde, from personal airplanes like the Cessna Skyhawk and the Beechcraft Bonanza to modern business jets like the Cessna Citation and the Learjet, from vintage P-51 Mustangs to homebuilts like the Rutan Vari-Eze and the world-class Voyager. If you pay your dues and become a member of the EAA, you can walk along the flight line, look at the airplanes, and watch the late afternoon airshows overhead. You can also talk with the owners and pilots and tap their knowledge about the aircraft and activities that interest you most.

At Oshkosh, it is sometimes possible to mingle with celebrities from the world of aviation as well. Famous pilots like Neil Armstrong, the first man to walk on the moon; Dick Rutan and Jeana Yeager, who flew nonstop around the world; Marsha Ivins, a NASA astronaut and safety specialist; and Captain John Cook, Concorde flight training manager for British Airways, are a few of the many respected pilots who often attend.

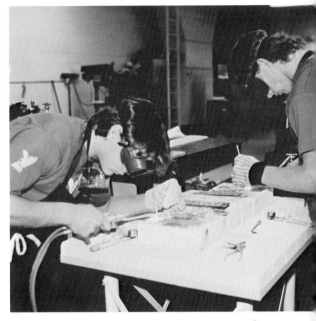

At the Air Academy, students learn aircraft design and construction methods.

Opportunities for Students

If you are interested in flying, information on any and every aspect of aviation is at the Fly-In for the asking. If you are interested in pursuing a career in aviation, for example, the Future Aviation Professionals of America (FAPA) staff an exhibit of books, magazines, and videos for aspiring pilots, mechanics, electronic technicians, flight attendants, and airport managers.

The EAA has recently developed a program for high school students aged 15 through 17 called Air Academy. For three weeks in the summer, about 36 young men and women can attend classes at the EAA Museum near Wittman Field and learn about aviation history and airplane design and construction methods. The Air Academy's graduation ceremonies are held during the Fly-In. A similar once-a-week program called Super Saturdays is sponsored by local EAA chapters throughout the country.

AN INVITATION

More and more high school students are becoming directly involved in the science and excitement of aviation. Aerospace science classes help students learn about science as they learn about flying. Madison's Memorial High School offers an aerospace science course for juniors and seniors. For students like yourself, a course like this provides an excellent opportunity to become involved in flying.

Teaming with Teachers

As the semester begins, members of Memorial High's aerospace science class take a 20-minute introductory flight in a Cessna 172 Skyhawk. After departing from Morey Airport and heading out around Madison's lakes, they

Many pilots begin to fly during high school. The Experimental Aircraft Association sponsors a summer Air Academy (left), and some high schools offer aviation classes.

get some first impressions about how exciting it can be to fly an airplane. Before and after the flight, instructors take time to answer questions and show students the various systems inside the cockpit.

Back in the classroom, teachers help students use desktop computers to learn the basics of flight planning and cross-country flight. Students also learn to use a hand-held flight computer to solve navigational problems quickly and easily. As the students learn about flying, they also study geography, physics, chemistry, biology, and math. Perhaps most importantly, they see how all these areas of academic knowledge can come together into a meaningful whole—safe, exciting flight.

The aerospace science class also features field trips that include a visit to the control tower and approach/departure control facility at Madison's Truax Field. Also on the agenda is a two-hour cross-country flight to two outlying airports, one of which has a control tower. While an instructor flies the airplane on takeoff and landing, three students plan the trip and fly one leg each. A trip to the EAA Museum provides a final highlight to a course

that generates a lot of enthusiasm in teachers and students alike.

Being Inner-Directed

You can, of course, learn about flying without an aerospace science course. You can continue reading about flying in books and magazines. You can write the aviation organizations listed on page 73 and find out about the services they provide.

Finally, of course, there is the flight school at your local airport. Earn some money and take a 20-minute, introductory lesson with a flight instructor. Ask your parents' permission ahead of time, and invite them along for the ride. Your first flight will help you see whether or not you want to work toward a private pilot's license of your own. If you do, and the flying bug bites hard enough, your interest may lead you to an aviation career that lasts a lifetime.

RESOURCES FOR FUTURE AVIATION PROFESSIONALS

Academy of Model Aeronautics
1810 Samuel Morse Drive
Reston, VA 22090

Aerospace Industries
Association of America
1250 I Street NW
Washington, DC 20005

Aircraft Electronics Association
P.O. Box 1981
Independence, MO 64055

Aircraft Owners and Pilots
Association
421 Aviation Way
Frederick, MD 21701

Airline Pilots Association
1625 Massachusetts Avenue NW
Washington, DC 20036

Air Traffic Control Association
2020 N. 14th Street Suite 410
Arlington, VA 22201

Center for Aerospace Sciences
University of North Dakota
P.O. Box 8216, University Station
Grand Forks, ND 58202

Experimental Aircraft
Association
Wittman Airfield
Oshkosh, WI 54903

Federal Aviation Administration
800 Independence Avenue SW
Washington, DC 20591

Future Aviation Professionals
of America
4959 Massachusetts Boulevard
Atlanta, GA 30337

National Association of
Flight Instructors
Ohio State University Airport
P.O. Box 20204
Columbus, OH 43220

National Intercollegiate
Flying Association
4627 Ocean Boulevard #220
San Diego, CA 92109

Society of Flight Test
Engineers
P.O. Box 4047
Lancaster, CA 93539

The following organizations also have aviation curriculum guides for teachers:

Aerospace Science Course
Memorial High School
201 South Gamma Road
Madison, WI 53717

Beech Aircraft Corporation
P.O. Box 85
Wichita, KS 67201

Cessna Aircraft Company
6330 West Southwest Boulevard
Wichita, KS 67215

Federal Aviation Administration
Great Lakes Region
2300 East Devon Avenue
Des Plaines, IL 60018

University Aviation Association
Auburn University
3410 Skyway Drive
Opelika, AL 36801

Wisconsin Department of
Transportation
4802 Sheboygan Avenue
Madison, WI 53702

FOR FURTHER READING

Bendick, Jeanne. *Airplanes*. New York: Franklin Watts, 1982.

Berger, Gilda. *Aviation: A Reference First Book*. New York: Franklin Watts, 1988.

Berliner, Don. *Distance Flights*. Minneapolis: Lerner Publications, 1990.

_____. *Personal Airplanes*. Minneapolis: Lerner Publications, 1982.

Pelta, Kathy. *What Does An Airline Pilot Do?* New York: Dodd, Mead & Company, 1981.

Rutland, Jonathan. *See Inside An Airport*. New York: Warwick Press, 1988.

Select Periodicals

AOPA Pilot
421 Aviation Way
Frederick, MD 21701

Air Progress
7950 Deering Avenue
Canoga Park, CA 91304

Flying
1515 Broadway
New York, NY 10036

Private Pilot
P.O. Box 6050
Mission Viejo, CA 92690

Plane and Pilot
16000 Ventura Boulevard Suite 800
Encino, CA 91436-2782

GLOSSARY

aileron A hinged section on the back edge of an airplane's wing that can be raised or lowered. The ailerons are used for banking the wings when making turns.

airspeed The speed at which the airplane travels through a body of air

airspeed indicator An instrument that measures airspeed

air traffic control (ATC) A system that guides airplane pilots when they are taking off, climbing, cruising, approaching, and landing

airway science A college program that prepares students for work in the aviation industry

air work Practicing basic maneuvers such as stalls, climbs, glides, turns, and slow flight

altimeter An instrument that indicates an aircraft's altitude

altitude The elevation of an airplane, either above sea level or above ground level

attitude indicator An instrument used to keep an airplane's wings level, or at a specific angle

automatic terminal information service (ATIS) A recording broadcast by some control towers that gives pilots weather, radio, and runway information for approach and departure

autopilot A device used in some airplanes that operates the flight controls while the pilot attends to navigation and watches for other aircraft

base leg The last leg in the airport traffic pattern before the final approach. The base leg is at a right angle to the runway.

centrifugal force The force that pushes pilots back and down into their seats when they change direction

climb An increase in an airplane's height, or altitude, above sea level

communication radio A radio used for spoken communication with air traffic controllers or instructors

control tower A facility from which air traffic controllers monitor ground and air traffic within 5 miles (8 kilometers) of an airport

control yoke A U-shaped arm that banks an airplane's wings when it is turned. The control yoke also raises or lowers the airplane's nose when it is pulled back or pushed forward.

dual instruction Time spent in an airplane taking lessons with an instructor

elevator A hinged surface on an airplane's tail that controls the upward and downward pitch of the airplane. Lowering the elevators causes the airplane to descend. Raising the elevators causes the airplane to climb.

flap A hinged appendage on an airplane's wing that can be raised or lowered to change the airplane's speed during landings

flight computer A hand-held calculator used to compute navigation, aircraft performance, and weight-and-balance calculations

flight engineer The pilot in charge of the engine, electrical, fuel, and hydraulic systems in a jet transport

flight simulator A machine that simulates the conditions a pilot might experience during actual flight

frequency In aviation, any radio setting between 108 and 136 megahertz that is used for navigation or communication

glide Decrease an airplane's height, or altitude, above the ground

ground school Classroom instruction that teaches about weather, navigation, airplane performance, air traffic control, and other subjects of importance to pilots

ground speed The speed at which an airplane travels over the ground. The speed can be lessened by headwinds or increased by tailwinds.

heading A direction that an airplane is pointed in reference to the magnetic compass

head-up display (HUD) A transparent screen, connected to computers, on which military pilots can read navigation and weapons information while looking out at the aircraft and environment around them

instrument flight rules (IFR) Rules that govern how pilots must fly when the cloud ceiling is less than 1,000 feet (300 meters) and the visibility is less than 3 miles (4.8 kilometers)—that is, when the weather is poor

instrument landing system (ILS) A radio facility that helps pilots line up precisely with the runway during their final approach

instrument rating The FAA's recognition that a pilot is qualified to fly safely by referring to instruments and radios alone

lift The upward force created when a wing is pulled through the air

navigation radio A radio that receives signals sent out by ground stations, such as VORs. With the navigation radio tuned to a particular ground station's frequency, a pilot can determine whether he or she is flying on course.

pitot tube A tube that measures the pressure caused by an airplane's forward movement. This measurement gives an airspeed reading on the aircraft's airspeed indicator.

propellor A device on an airplane engine with two or more blades that extend from a central shaft. When a propellor spins rapidly, it either pulls or pushes the airplane through the air.

radar A system that uses reflected radio waves to detect the presence of airplanes and various kinds of weather. Air traffic controllers use radar to guide airplanes in their area. Pilots may use radar to locate storms and other aircraft.

radio course A radio signal sent out from a VOR station that helps guide pilots to and from the station

rudder A vertical piece of the tail that is used to push the airplane's nose to the left or right during a turn

sectional chart A map for pilots that shows landmarks, airports, and VOR stations

short-field takeoffs and landings Techniques that allow pilots to take off and land on short runways

slow flight Reducing power and speed, yet staying at the same altitude by raising the airplane's nose

stall An aircraft stalls, or quits flying, when the wing is not pulled through the air fast enough to create lift.

taxi To move the airplane on the ground by starting the engine and steering with the rudder pedals

throttle A control handle that increases engine power when pushed forward and decreases engine power when pulled backward

TO-FROM indicator An instrument connected to a navigation radio that tells when an airplane is on course as it flies to or from a VOR

traffic pattern A rectangular path around an airport runway that pilots must follow as they take off, depart, approach, and land

unicom A small radio transmitter that provides pilots with local weather information and allows them to talk with one another

vector An aircraft heading assigned by air traffic control

VFR minimums The minimum visibility and cloud ceiling in which pilots may fly by visual flight rules

visual flight rules (VFR) Rules that govern how pilots should fly when the cloud ceiling is above 1,000 feet (300 m) and visibility is 3 miles (4.8 km) or greater —that is, when the weather is fair to good

VOR A very high frequency omnidirectional range station. The VOR station sends out radio signals that pilots use to navigate during cross-country flight.

INDEX

ACKNOWLEDGMENTS The photographs in this book are reproduced through the courtesy of: Tom Zwemke, Cessna Aircraft Company: pp. 2, 8, 17, 19, 24, 27, 28, 30, 45, 51, 54; Carter M. Ayres: pp. 6, 15 (top), 26, 35, 36, 39, 44, 53; Gordon Perkins and Jim Hein: pp. 9, 10, 11, 15, (bottom), 16, 19, 22, 23, 31, 32, 80; Roger J. Ritchie, FlightSafety International Inc.: pp. 18, 46, 48, 50; Federal Aviation Administration: pp. 29 (Lance Strozier), 34 (Michael McKean), 37 (Ken Gustin); Patty McClain, FlightSafety International Inc.: pp. 40, 44, 47, 52, 55, 56; United States Navy: pp. 41 (Joc Rich Beth), 60 (Douglas E. Houser), 63 (Alex C. Hicks), 65 (McDonnell Douglas), 61, 62, 64; United Airlines: pp. 43, 58; Experimental Aircraft Association: pp. 66, 67 (Jeffrey Isom), 68, 69, 70 (Jim Koepnick), 71 (Carl Schuppel). Stoddard-Hamilton Aircraft, Inc.: p. 79. Cover photographs courtesy of Jim Koepnick, Experimental Aircraft Association (front cover, right), Gordon Perkins and Jim Hein (front cover, left; back cover). Illustrations by Laura Westlund.